Hello, my name is Clancy.

My name is ____________________________.

I am in Year __________.

My teacher is ____________________________.

Track your progress

As you complete pages in this book, trace over the matching letter here.

OXFORD UNIVERSITY PRESS

as in “six”

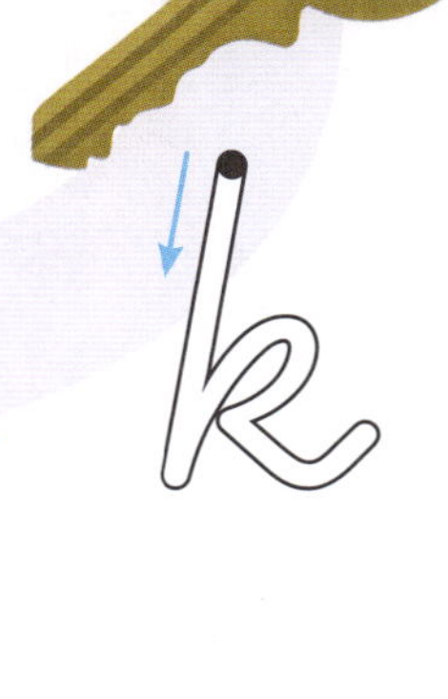

Before you begin writing ...

Here are the 3Ps that will help you with your writing: posture, pencil grip and paper position. You will be reminded about these as you work through the book.

Posture

- Relax your arms.
- Sit back in your chair.
- Make sure your back is straight.
- Put your feet flat on the floor.

Pencil grip

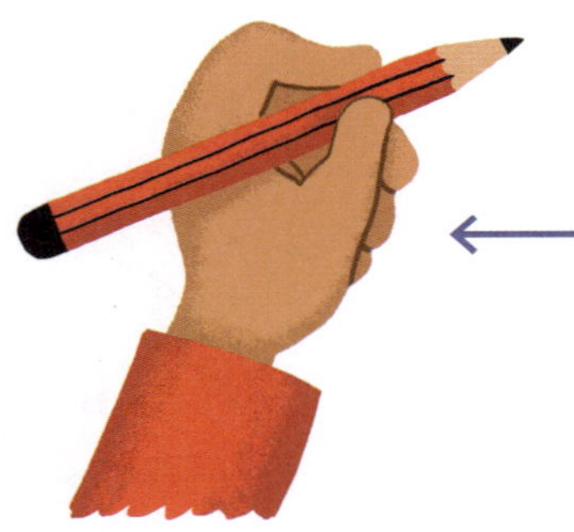

Hold your pencil like this. (Not too tightly!)

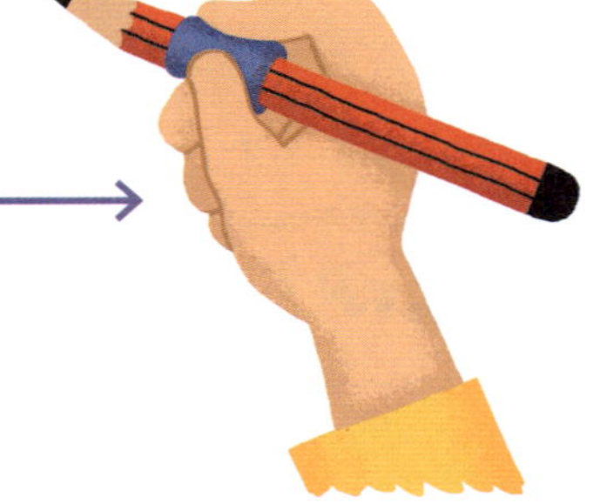

Left-handed

Right-handed

Paper position

Use your non-writing hand to steady the paper.

Left-handed

Right-handed

Hand and finger warm-ups

Crocodile snaps (whole arms)

Start with one arm straight above the head and the other extended down one side of the body. Snap the hands together, like a crocodile snapping its jaws. Repeat, but reverse the arms.

Open, shut them. (hands)

Open, shut them. Open, shut them.
Give a little clap!
Open, shut them. Open, shut them.
Lay them in your lap.
Repeat.

Spider push-ups (fingers)

Place the fingertips together and bend and straighten the fingers while pushing the fingertips against each other.

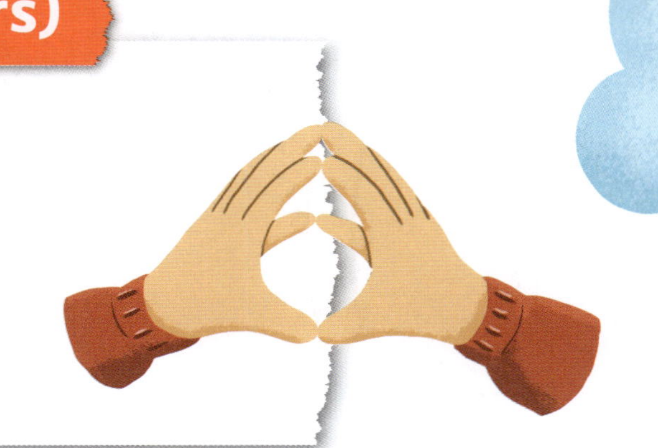

Warm-up patterns for anti-clockwise letters

Trace the patterns.

Trace and then continue each pattern.

Create your own anti-clockwise patterns.

above
on
below

a a

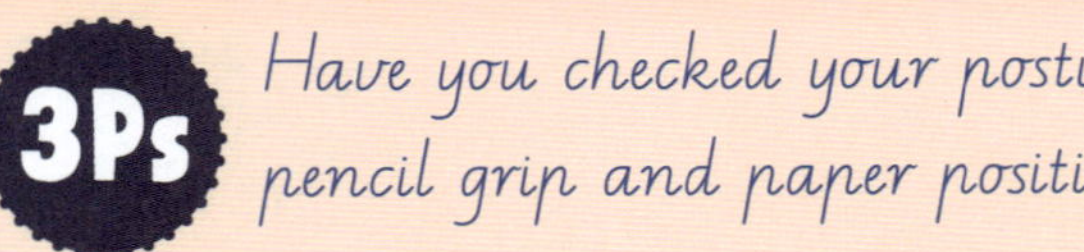

3Ps

Have you checked your posture, pencil grip and paper position?

Have you done your warm-ups?

avocado

Trace and then copy the letters and words.

a a a a a a a a a a

a

at all are

at

arrive arrives arrived

arrive

ask asks asking

ask

act acts acted action

act

Self-assessment

Put a circle around your best letter and word on each page.
Explain your choice to your teacher or classmate.

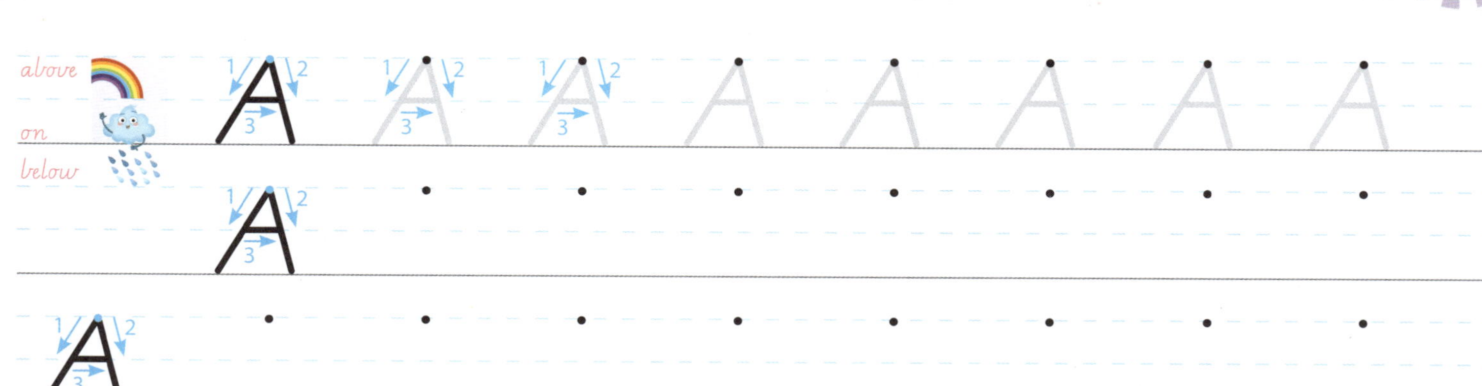

Ali arrived at the Acropolis

Ali

at exactly the right time today.

at

Write a sentence including words with the letter a on the lines below.

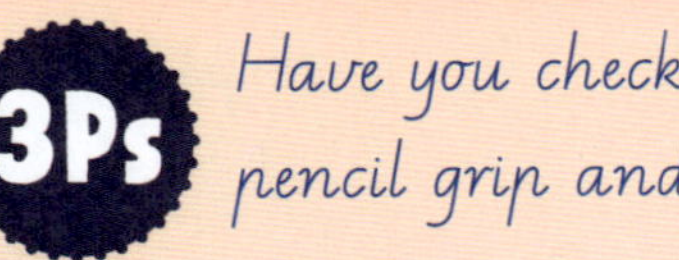

Have you checked your posture, pencil grip and paper position?

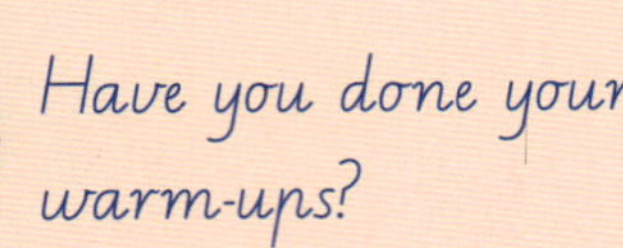

Have you done your warm-ups?

Trace and then copy the letters and words.

c c c c c c c c c c

c

can cannot can't

can

cook cooking cooked

cook

close closed closing

close

call calls called

call

Self-assessment Put a circle around your best letter and word on each page. Explain your choice to your teacher or classmate.

above
on
below

c c c c c c c c
c
c

Cara cooked a creamy coconut
Cara

cake for her cousin Chad.
cake

Write a sentence including words with the letter c on the lines below.

Have you checked your posture, pencil grip and paper position?

Have you done your warm-ups?

drums

Trace and then copy the letters and words.

d d d d d d d d d d

d

dry dries drying

dry

did did not didn't

did

dislike dislikes disliked

dislike

dance dances danced

dance

Self-assessment

Put a circle around your best letter and word on each page.
Explain your choice to your teacher or classmate.

OXFORD UNIVERSITY PRESS

above
on
below

D D D D D D D D
D
D

Dusty the dog was dirty when he
Dusty
came out of the muddy puddle!
came

Write a sentence including words with the letter d on the lines below.

Have you checked your posture, pencil grip and paper position?

Have you done your warm-ups?

grapes

Trace and then copy the letters and words.

g g g g g g g g g g

g

go going gone

go

gleam gleams gleaming

gleam

grace gracious graceful

grace

glide glides glided

glide

Self-assessment

Put a circle around your best letter and word on each page. Explain your choice to your teacher or classmate.

Gino, go and get the green lead.

Gino

We are going to Gray's park.

We

Write a sentence including words with the letter g on the lines below.

Have you checked your posture, pencil grip and paper position?

Have you done your warm-ups?

quilt

Trace and then copy the letters and words.

q q q q q q q q q q

q

quiet quieter quietest

quiet

quick quicker quickest

quick

quokka quail quoll

quokka

quack quacks quacked

quack

Self-assessment

Put a circle around your best letter and word on each page.
Explain your choice to your teacher or classmate.

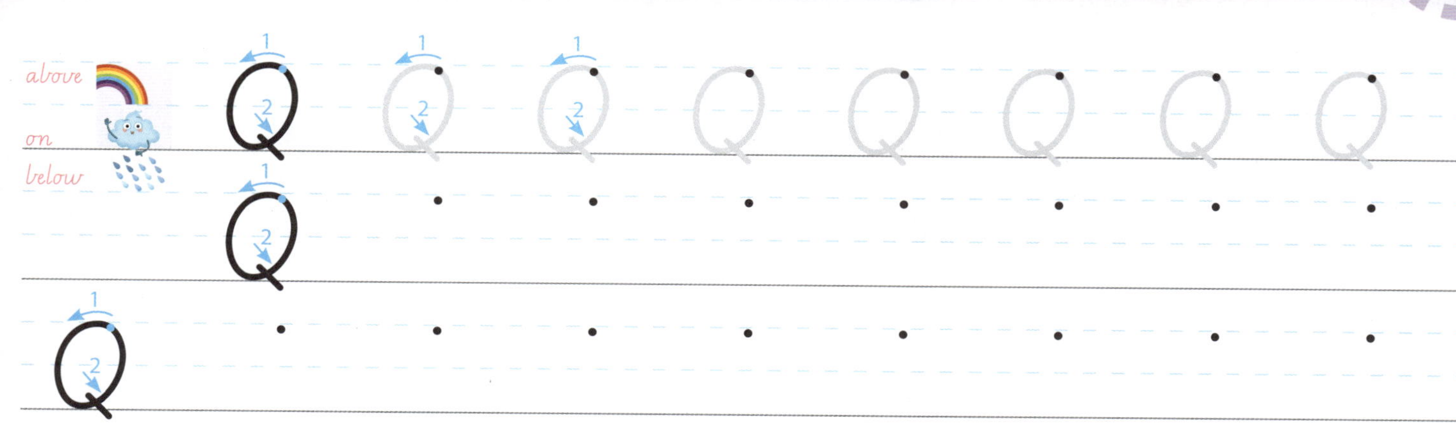

Queenie the quoll moves quickly

Queenie

and quietly past the quokka.

and

Write a sentence including words with the letter q on the lines below.

Have you checked your posture, pencil grip and paper position?

Have you done your warm-ups?

echidna

Trace and then copy the letters and words.

e e e e e e e e e e

e

eat eats eaten

eat

excite exciting excited

excite

eight eighteen eighth

eight

ensure ensures ensured

ensure

Self-assessment

Put a circle around your best letter and word on each page.
Explain your choice to your teacher or classmate.

OXFORD UNIVERSITY PRESS

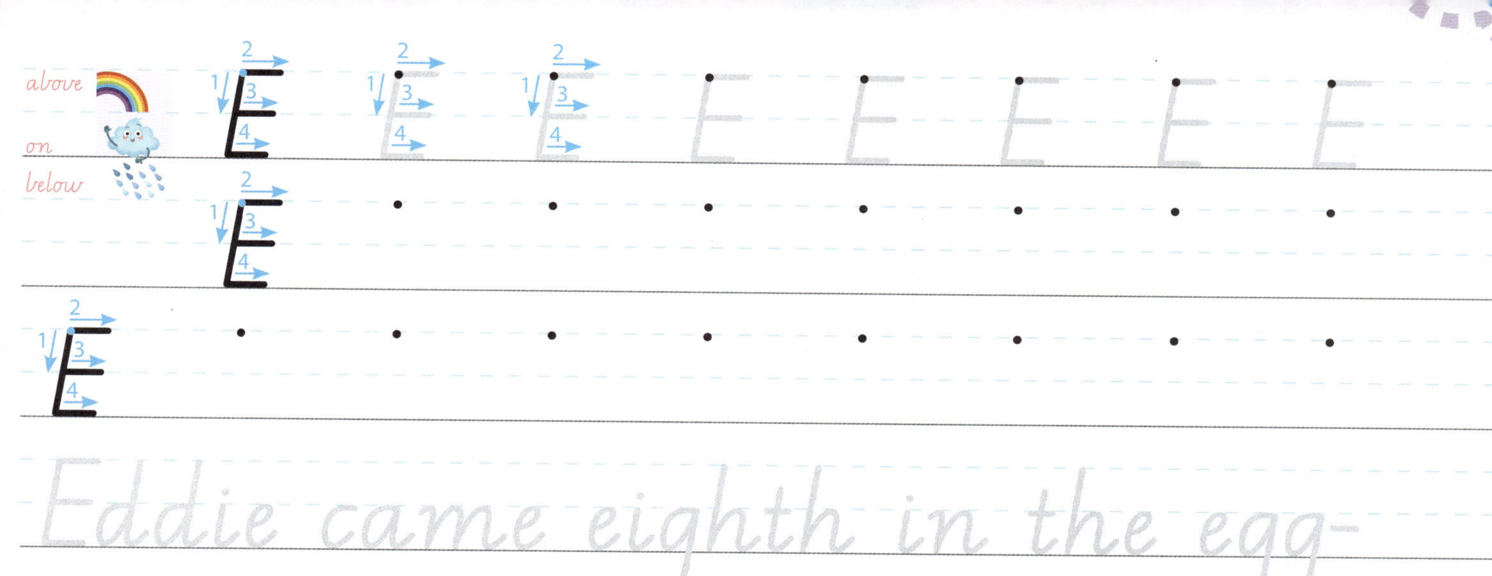

Eddie came eighth in the egg-
Eddie
and-spoon race on sports day.
and

Write a sentence including words with the letter e on the lines below.

Have you checked your posture, pencil grip and paper position?

Have you done your warm-ups?

octopus

Trace and then copy the letters and words.

o o o o o o o o o o

o

on off out over

on

open opening opened

open

only outside orange

only

order orders ordered

order

Self-assessment

Put a circle around your best letter and word on each page. Explain your choice to your teacher or classmate.

OXFORD UNIVERSITY PRESS

above
on
below

O

O

O

Olivia and I opened all of our

Olivia

birthday presents at once!

birthday

Write a sentence including words with the letter o on the lines below.

Have you checked your posture, pencil grip and paper position?

Have you done your warm-ups?

floaty

Trace and then copy the letters and words.

f f f f f f f f f f

f

float floats floating

float

fly flying flew

fly

friend friends friendly

friend

flow flows flowed

flow

Self-assessment

Put a circle around your best letter and word on each page. Explain your choice to your teacher or classmate.

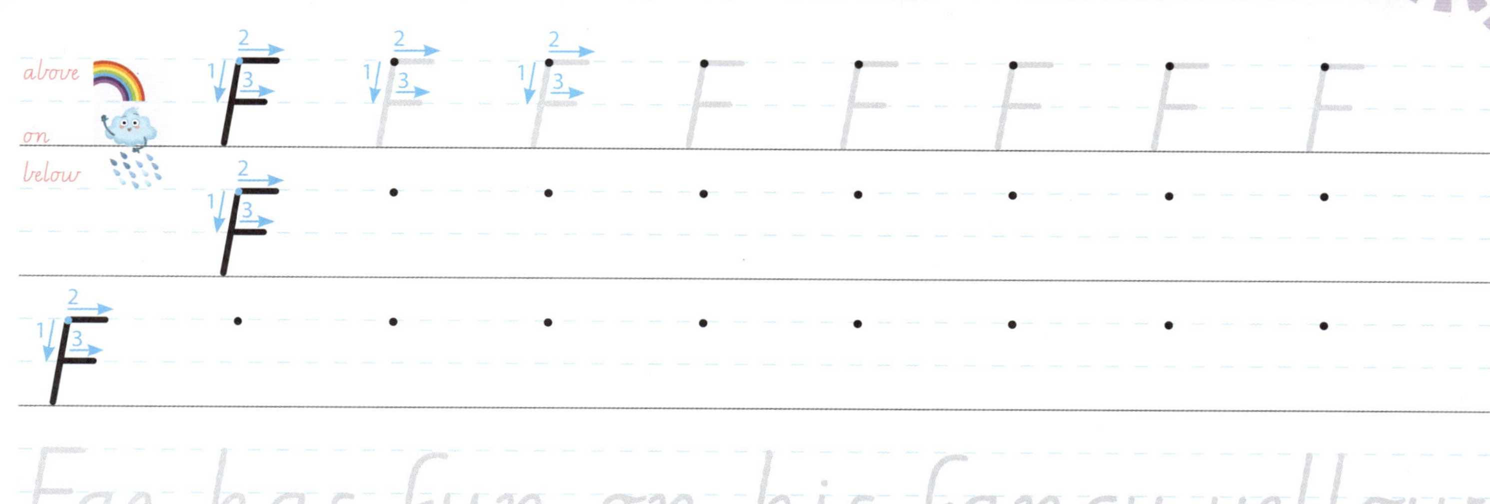

Faz has fun on his fancy yellow

Faz

floaty. His dad watches him.

floaty

Write a sentence including words with the letter f on the lines below.

above
on
below

Have you checked your posture, pencil grip and paper position?

Have you done your warm-ups?

submarine

Trace and then copy the letters and words.

s s s s s s s s s s

s

sleep sleeping slept

sleep

silly sillier silliest

silly

some someone something

some

save saves saved

save

Teacher comment

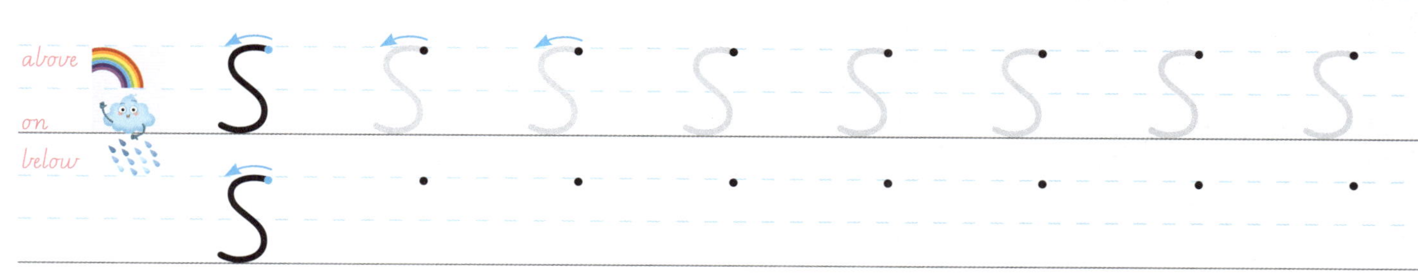

Sami slept in on Sunday and

Sami

was late for the soccer game.

was

Write a sentence including words with the letter s on the lines below.

Warm-up patterns for clockwise letters

Trace the patterns.

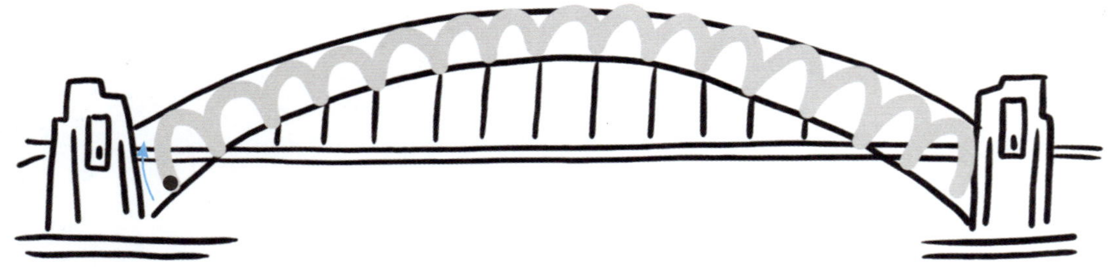

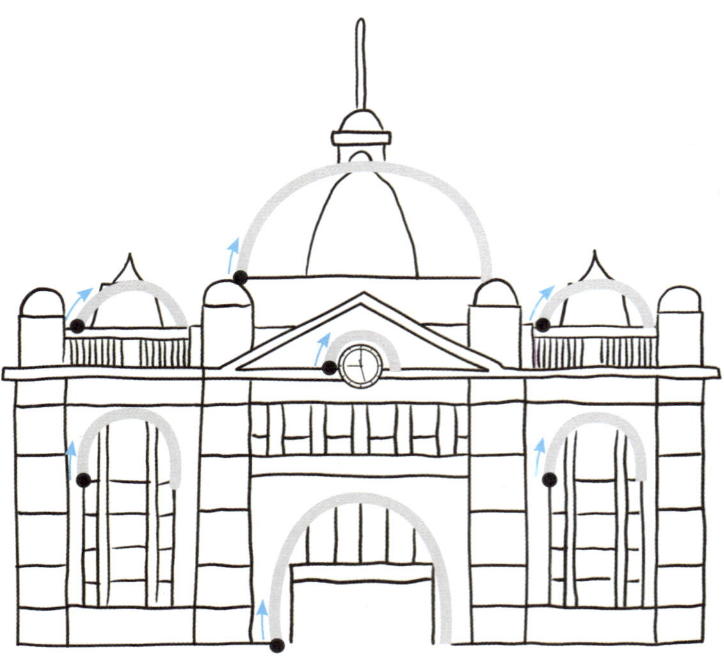

Trace and then continue each pattern.

Create your own clockwise patterns.

Have you checked your posture, pencil grip and paper position?

Have you done your warm-ups?

Trace and then copy the letters and words.

m m m m m m m m m m

m

makes making made

m

may monkey march

m

magic magical magically

m

miss misses missed

m

Self-assessment

Put a circle around your best letter and word on each page. Explain your choice to your teacher or classmate.

OXFORD UNIVERSITY PRESS

above
on
below

M M M M M M M M

M

M

Max and Malia played melodic

M

music at the school concert.

m

Write a sentence including words with the letter m on the lines below.

Have you checked your posture, pencil grip and paper position?

Have you done your warm-ups?

Trace and then copy the letters and words.

n n n n n n n n n n

n

new newer newest

n

nice nicer nicest

n

nine ninth nineteen

n

note notes noted

n

Self-assessment

Put a circle around your best letter and word on each page. Explain your choice to your teacher or classmate.

OXFORD UNIVERSITY PRESS

Nick and his family want to see

N

the new film that starts at nine.

t

Write a sentence including words with the letter n on the lines below.

Have you checked your posture, pencil grip and paper position?

Have you done your warm-ups?

Trace and then copy the letters and words.

r r r r r r r r r r

r

run running ran

r

rain rainbow rainforest

r

refuse refuses refused

r

relax relaxes relaxed

r

Self-assessment

Put a circle around your best letter and word on each page. Explain your choice to your teacher or classmate.

above
on
below

R R R R R R R R

R

R

Rollo saw a bright rainbow over

R

the lush, tropical rainforest.

t

Write a sentence including words with the letter r on the lines below.

Have you checked your posture, pencil grip and paper position?

Have you done your warm-ups?

x as in "six"

Trace and then copy the letters and words.

x x x x x x x x x x

box fox next six

b

mix fix vex ox

m

explore explores explored

e

excite excites excited

e

Self-assessment

Put a circle around your best letter and word on each page.
Explain your choice to your teacher or classmate.

Mr X, the excited little fox,

explores a complex rabbit hole.

Write a sentence including words with the letter x on the lines below.

Have you checked your posture, pencil grip and paper position?

Have you done your warm-ups?

Trace and then copy the letters and words.

z z z z z z z z z z

z

zip zipper zigzag

z

lazy laziest laziness

l

puzzle puzzles puzzled

p

zoom zooms zoomed

z

Self-assessment Put a circle around your best letter and word on each page. Explain your choice to your teacher or classmate.

OXFORD UNIVERSITY PRESS

above

on

below

z z z z z z z z

z

z

Zahra's popcorn, pizza and

Z

puzzle party was amazing!

p

Write a sentence including words with the letter z on the lines below.

Have you checked your posture, pencil grip and paper position?

Have you done your warm-ups?

helicopter

Trace and then copy the letters and words.

h h h h h h h h h h

h

help helping helped

h

heap heaps heaped

h

happy happiest happily

h

hollow hollows hollowed

h

Self-assessment

Put a circle around your best letter and word on each page. Explain your choice to your teacher or classmate.

OXFORD UNIVERSITY PRESS

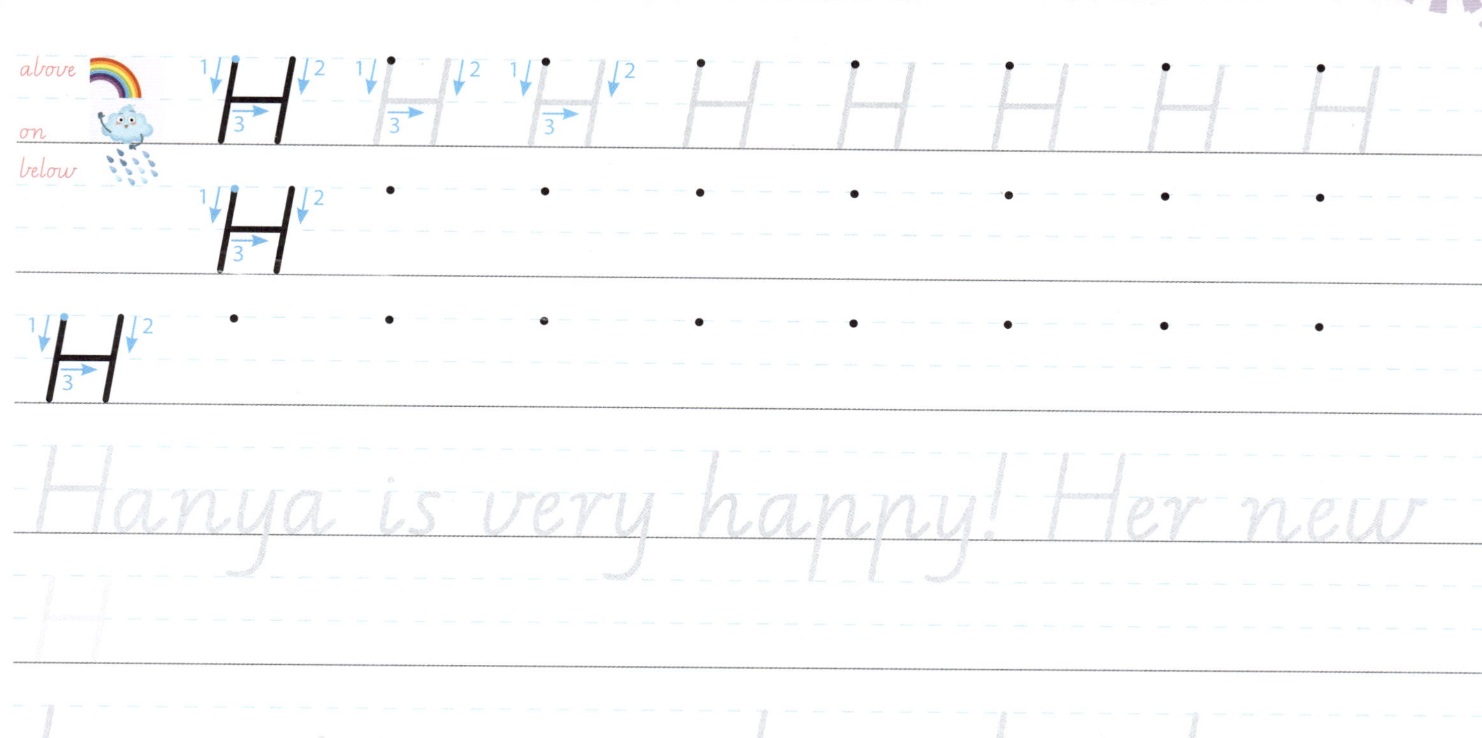

Write a sentence including words with the letter h on the lines below.

Have you checked your posture, pencil grip and paper position?

Have you done your warm-ups?

key

Trace and then copy the letters and words.

k k k k k k k k k k

k

kicks kicking kicked

k

know knows known

k

kangaroo koala kookaburra

k

keep keeps kept

k

Self-assessment

Put a circle around your best letter and word on each page.
Explain your choice to your teacher or classmate.

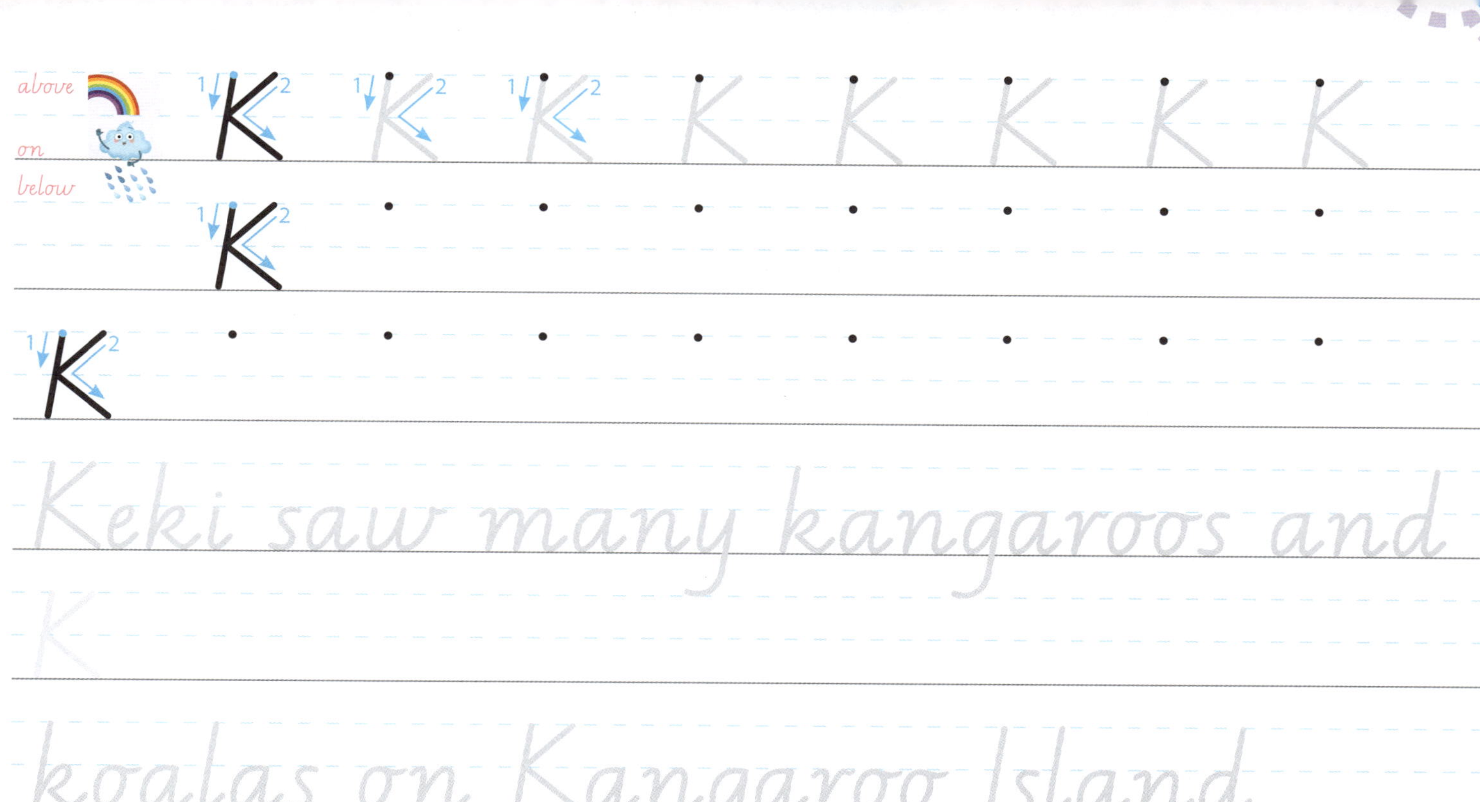

Write a sentence including words with the letter k on the lines below.

above
on
below

p p

Have you checked your posture, pencil grip and paper position?

Have you done your warm-ups?

paint

Trace and then copy the letters and words.

p p p p p p p p p p

p

play plays playing played

p

pancake popcorn pineapple

p

paper page patch picture

p

perform performs performed

p

Teacher comment

above
on
below

p p p p p p p p

p

p

Pete's band performed in the

p

playground for the parents.

p

Write a sentence including words with the letter p on the lines below.

Warm-up patterns for i and u family letters

Trace the patterns.

Trace and then continue each pattern.

Create your own patterns.

Have you checked your posture, pencil grip and paper position?

Have you done your warm-ups?

Trace and then copy the letters and words.

i i i i i i i i i i

i

in if it is

i

into inside include

i

invent invents invention

i

invite invites invited

i

Self-assessment

Put a circle around your best letter and word on each page. Explain your choice to your teacher or classmate.

OXFORD UNIVERSITY PRESS

above
on
below

I imagined that I invented an

incredible dancing robot.

Write a sentence including words with the letter i on the lines below.

Have you checked your posture, pencil grip and paper position?

Have you done your warm-ups?

Trace and then copy the letters and words.

t t t t t t t t t t

t

take takes taking

t

think thinks thinking

t

today tomorrow yesterday

t

toot toots tooted

t

Self-assessment

Put a circle around your best letter and word on each page. Explain your choice to your teacher or classmate.

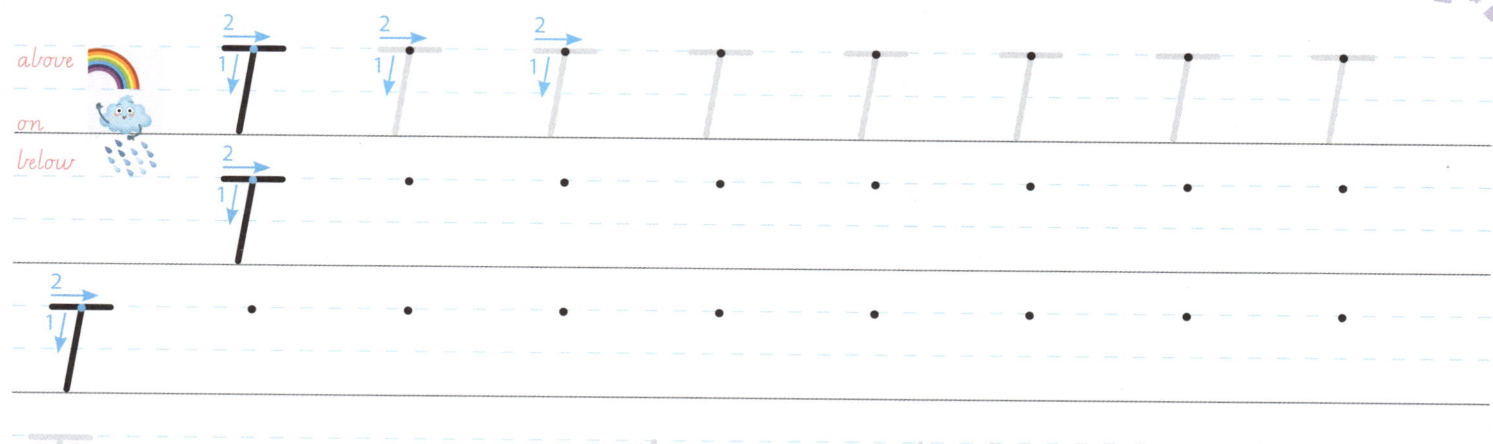

Tam is excited to celebrate his

tenth birthday and eat treats!

Write a sentence including words with the letter t on the lines below.

Have you checked your posture, pencil grip and paper position?

Have you done your warm-ups?

lips

Trace and then copy the letters and words.

l l l l l l l l l l

l

live lives living lived

l

love loves loving loved

l

limb light line loan

l

like likes liked

l

Self-assessment

Put a circle around your best letter and word on each page. Explain your choice to your teacher or classmate.

OXFORD UNIVERSITY PRESS

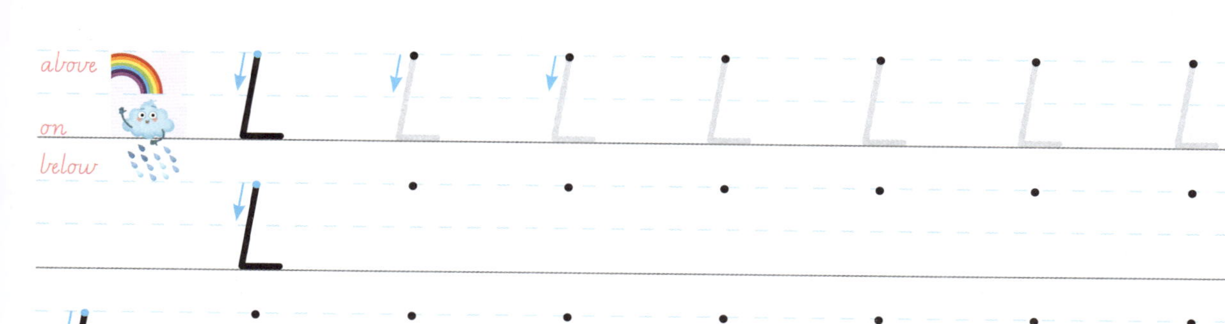

Lia lives in Alice Springs with

l

her family and Lila the lizard.

h

Write a sentence including words with the letter l on the lines below.

Have you checked your posture, pencil grip and paper position?

Have you done your warm-ups?

jam

Trace and then copy the letters and words.

1 2. j j j j j j j j j j

1 2. j

joke joking joked

j

jump jumps jumping

j

jungle justice judge

j

join joins joined

j

Self-assessment

Put a circle around your best letter and word on each page.
Explain your choice to your teacher or classmate.

above
on
below

j j j j j j j j
j
j

Jill wears her jumper in July
J

but is still shaking like jelly.
b

Write a sentence including words with the letter j on the lines below.

Have you checked your posture, pencil grip and paper position?

Have you done your warm-ups?

Trace and then copy the letters and words.

u u u u u u u u u u

u

use uses using

u

undo undone undoing

u

underground unsteady usually

u

unpack unpacks unpacked

u

Self-assessment Put a circle around your best letter and word on each page. Explain your choice to your teacher or classmate.

above
on
below

u u u u u u u u

u

u

Uri used his chunky crayons to

U

draw a picture for his mum.

d

Write a sentence including words with the letter u on the lines below.

Have you checked your posture, pencil grip and paper position?

Have you done your warm-ups?

Trace and then copy the letters and words.

y y y y y y y y y y

y

you your yours yourself

y

young younger youngest

y

yum yummy yummiest

y

yell yells yelled

y

Self-assessment

Put a circle around your best letter and word on each page. Explain your choice to your teacher or classmate.

OXFORD UNIVERSITY PRESS

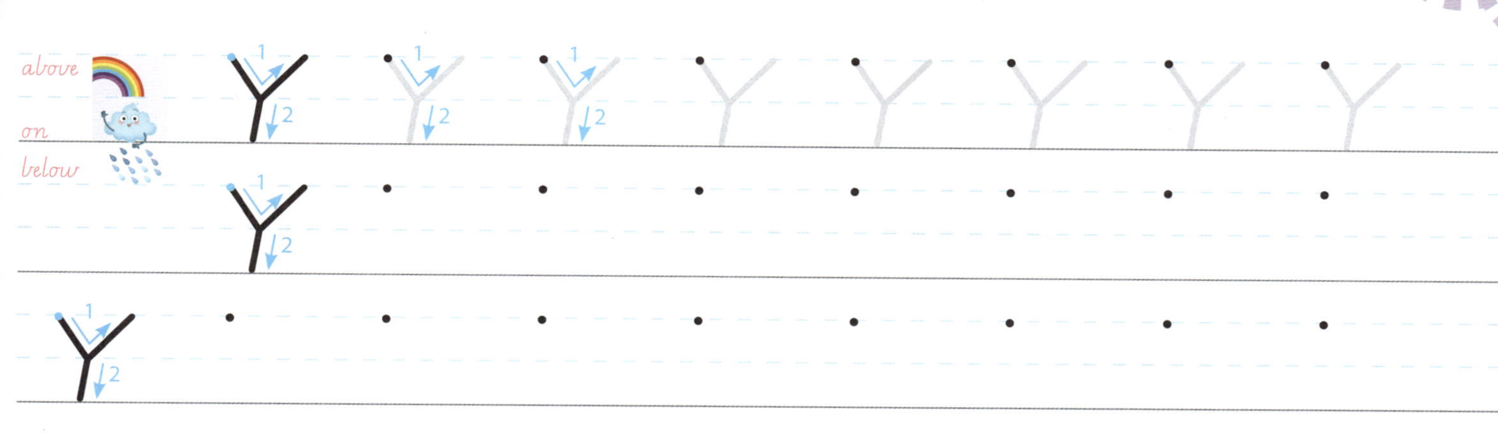

Yesterday, Yindi brought the

yummiest lunch to school.

Write a sentence including words with the letter y on the lines below.

Have you checked your posture, pencil grip and paper position?

Have you done your warm-ups?

vegetables

Trace and then copy the letters and words.

v v v v v v v v v v

v

visit visits visitors

v

everyone everybody everyday

e

vary varied various

v

veer veers veered

v

Self-assessment

Put a circle around your best letter and word on each page. Explain your choice to your teacher or classmate.

OXFORD UNIVERSITY PRESS

above
on
below

v v v v v v v v v

v

v

Vicky and her family saw

v

vultures fly over the valley.

v

Write a sentence including words with the letter v on the lines below.

Have you checked your posture, pencil grip and paper position?

Have you done your warm-ups?

Trace and then copy the letters and words.

w w w w w w w w w w

w

want wants wanted

w

walk walking walked

w

water watering watered

w

watch watches watched

w

Self-assessment

Put a circle around your best letter and word on each page. Explain your choice to your teacher or classmate.

Write a sentence including words with the letter w on the lines below.

Have you checked your posture, pencil grip and paper position?

Have you done your warm-ups?

Trace and then copy the letters and words.

b b b b b b b b b b

b

big bigger biggest

b

break breaks breaking

b

behind below before

b

bake bakes baked

b

Teacher comment

Benjamin saw the biggest spider

B

climbing behind the bench!

c

Write a sentence including words with the letter b on the lines below.

Trace and then copy the lower- and upper-case letters.

aA bB cC dD eE

fF gG hH iI jJ kK

lL mM nN oO pP

qQ rR sS tT uU

vV wW xX yY zZ

Trace and copy the numbers.

1 2 3 4 5

6 7 8 9 10

Teacher comment